The Busy Teacher's Guide to *Macbeth*

A QUICK GUIDE TO EVERYTHING YOUR STUDENTS NEED TO KNOW

Heather Wright

Saugeen Publishing

Kitchener, Ontario

Heather Wright
Kitchener, Ontario, Canada
http://wrightingwords.com

The Busy Teacher's Guide to Teaching *Macbeth*/ Heather Wright.
—1st ed.

ISBN-13: 978-1515031635

ISBN-10: 1515031632

Contents

Dedicated to the Teachers!

"You can't stop a teacher when they want to do something. They just do it."

—— J.D. Salinger, The Catcher in the Rye

CHAPTER 1

The Essentials

These are the notes you wish that the previous teacher had left behind—the basics that you need to get on with your job: scene summaries, homework questions, backgrounds to the play and Shakespeare's time, themes and essay topics.

Your teaching time is limited, but you want your students to get as much out of the text as possible in the short time in which you have to teach it. In your wildest dreams, you want them all to love it. At the least, (which isn't a small thing at all) you want them to feel like competent readers with the ability to take on a new text and find the keys to understanding it.

To help you find what you need, this book is organized into 7 sections:

1. Context – Where is the writer coming from? Shakespeare's England and how it affects the content of the play.
2. Key themes and images – What motifs does the writer use to develop the story?
3. Format/Genre – What are some basic rules about the kind of material I am teaching?
4. Scene-by-Scene – What do I need to explain to or bring out of my students as we read through this work? These sections are followed by some **handy homework questions** that you can assign the students while reading through the play. These questions are also available here for downloading and printing.
5. Topics for Journal Writing – How can I get students to think about a topic or a theme before they start reading? Assigning a journal topic can help. After they've explored an idea on their own, they often bring deeper insights to discussions.
6. The 5-paragraph essay - What essay topics can I assign for this play? Here are a few five-paragraph essay topics that you can use for summative evaluation or for an exam, along with **an essay-writing template, a sample essay, and links to evaluation rubrics**.
7. Online Resources – Where can I find more homework questions and answers, essay topics and creative projects for my students?

CHAPTER 2

Context

King James and the witches

By the time, Shakespeare writes *Macbeth*, King James has taken the throne, and Shakespeare's company has changed its name to the King's Men. Previously King James VI of Scotland, James I of England considered himself to be an intellectual and was eager to impress the cultured people of London. While King of Scotland, James wrote a book about witches, *Demonology*, and certainly, witches in those days were considered real and dangerous. While James was King of Scotland, many hundreds of women were executed as witches. You can read a lot more here: http://www.historylearningsite.co.uk/james-I-witchcraft.htm

Note in the above reference, that one of the events the witches were blamed for was a severe storm at sea that James encountered on the way back from a trip to Denmark. In the play, the witches cause terrible storms to harm a sailor whose wife didn't share her chestnuts with a witch.

Chain of Being

In Medieval and early Renaissance times, the world was considered to be complete and unchanging. Politically, socially and in nature, the world was organized into a hierarchy that looked like this.

God
Angels
Humans
Animals
Plants
Minerals

Within each of the above categories, there were also other hierarchies. Angels had their own order: Seraphim, Cherubim, Thrones, Dominions, Virtues, Powers, Archangels, Principalities, Angels.

The hierarchy of humans looks like this

King/Queen
Nobility
Middle Class

Lower Class

Peasants

There are three things to remember about this hierarchy.

1) People believed that the rulers were appointed by God.

2) If you were born into a particular level of the hierarchy, you were supposed to stay there and not take power away from the person who had the power above you.

3) If there is a serious disturbance to the hierarchy, the natural order will reflect that disturbance by changes in weather and in the behaviour of birds and animals.

You can read more about the Chain of Being here:

http://faculty.grandview.edu/ssnyder/121/121%20great%20chain.htm

---

The Real Macbeth

Here are some links to the history of the real Macbeth.

King Macbeth of Scotland (1040 - 1057) http://www.britroyals.com/scots.asp?id=macbeth

Macbeth 'the Red King' – Mac Bethad mac Findlaích (d. 1057)

http://www.educationscotland.gov.uk/scotlandshistory/makingthenation/macbeth/index.asp

There's no real evidence that Macbeth killed Duncan. Macbeth ruled for 17 years before he was killed in battle by Macduff, and was considered to be a pretty good king. The Scots had a habit of killing their kings. Here's a link to a list of Scottish kings, and you can see how long they actually reigned and how they died. http://www.rampantscotland.com/features/monarchs.htm

As a side note: King James is Scottish and a patron of Shakespeare's theatre company. He is an expert on witches and doesn't have much patience with short plays. He is also distantly related to the character of Banquo. Shakespeare clearly knew how to flatter a king and make sure that James continued to support his theatre. Politically correct, indeed!

CHAPTER 3

Format/Genre

In Renaissance theatre, all the roles were performed by men and boys, which explains why there aren't too many female roles in Shakespeare's plays. In a few of Shakespeare's plays (*Twelfth Night, Merchant of Venice*, for example) the female characters get to dress as young men for part of the play. These roles today are known as 'britches' roles.

Blank Verse, etc.

For the most part, in Shakespeare's plays, the noble characters speak in blank verse and the others speak in prose. Blank verse means that the lines the characters speak are written in iambic pentameter, with 10 beats per line. The ten beats are broken into 5 units or feet, each of which usually has a light beat followed by a heavy one—ta **dum**, ta **dum**, ta **dum**, ta **dum**, ta **dum**.

Rarely do two consecutive lines rhyme, except at the ends of the scenes.

Your students might not think that this all matters much, but it mattered a lot to the Elizabethan audience. They were a very aural society. They could detect the changes in speaking patterns from one character to the next. The plays were presented with very little furniture and no scenery. It was important for the audience to hear the rhyming couplet at the end of the scene so that they could prepare themselves for the new scene that they were going to see next. The chair that a person used as a throne in one scene could be part of a ship in the next or a rock in another. Since the scenery changed little, the dialogue had to tell the audience what it was supposed to imagine on the stage.

Blank verse also helped the actors. Memorizing poetry is always easier than memorizing prose. There are also clues in the way that the dialogue is written on the page that helps the actors know how to say their lines.

One clue occurs when the beats in the line don't follow the usual pattern. This break in the iambic pentameter rhythm, means that the actor has to emphasize words in that line differently that in the lines before or after. It's Shakespeare's way of making sure that a particular word gets the emphasis it should, so that it is picked up by the audience.

Another clue in the dialogue that helps actors is in the way the words physically appear on the script. Most of the actors were never given the complete script from which to learn their lines. They were given only their own lines written out along with the line that the person says before it's their turn (their cue), and the line that follows. These short excerpts of scripts were called "sides."

The way that the cue line and their first line is written gives the actors another clue about how to say their lines when they're speaking blank verse. Every complete line in blank verse has 10 beats. If, for example, the cue line has 5 beats and ends part way across the page, and the next character's line starts part way across the page and also has 5 beats, that tells the actor that he shouldn't pause after the previous speaker has finished speaking. He should "pick up the cue" right away. If, however, the cue line has 5 beats and ends part way across the page, but the next line has ten beats, then that means that the actor can take a short pause before he speaks his line to account for the five missing beats.

Near the end of Act 1, scene 6, Lines 65 to 71—The exchange between Lady Macbeth and Macbeth is written so that there are no pauses between their lines, giving the scene a sense of urgency. Lady Macbeth's line 72, "Shall sun that morrow see!" is only 6 beats long. There is a 4 beat pause where she sees Macbeth's reaction to what she has said about killing the king that night and figures out what to say to keep him from changing her plans. Then her next line, "Your face, my thane, is as a book where men/" is a full 10 beats.

Dramatic Irony

Dramatic irony occurs when the audience knows something that the characters don't. In *Macbeth*, Duncan and Macduff talk about what a lovely, safe haven Macbeth's castle appears to be and how they look forward to staying there. The audience knows that Macbeth and Lady Macbeth plan to murder Duncan that night, so the castle is hardly a safe haven for Duncan.

Aside

This is a theatre technique that doesn't happen a lot in modern theatre, but was very common in Shakespeare's time. In an aside, the actor speaks directly to the audience while there are other people on stage. Melodramas at the turn of the last century used this technique as well, and it was carried through into silent films. An example from *Macbeth* occurs in Act 1, scene 3 at line 140.

Soliloquy

In a soliloquy, the actor is alone on stage. He or she is not speaking directly to the audience, but rather, thinking out loud about how he or she feels about a problem in the play. Macbeth's speech in which he sees the dagger is a soliloquy. (Act 2, scene 1)

CHAPTER 4

Key Themes and Images

There are five key themes/images to remember while reading *Macbeth.*

1) Natural Order and the consequences of disrupting the natural order by killing a king.
2) Clothing Imagery
3) Fair is Foul
4) Illness and Disease
5) Tragic Hero

Having the students make note of these as they read through the text will help them build a selection of quotes that they can use for essays and projects based on these themes. If they can't write in their texts, students could use colour-coded sticky notes or pieces of paper or keep separate pages in their notes for each theme and write down the entire quote or at least the scene and line numbers. Your recording them on chart paper hanging in the room would help, too.

The class could also be broken into 5 groups, one for experts on each theme, and you could use the jigsaw method to share the expertise after you have finished going through the play. The expert groups could also do presentations for the class with handouts containing their key information.

Disruption of Natural Order.

The murder of a ruler and takeover by another nobleman is something that the Elizabethan/Jacobean audience would have taken very seriously. Their own history was full of civil war already with the Wars of the Roses (1455 - 1485) then the upheavals of the reign of Henry VIII, and the uncertainties of the reign of Elizabeth I, who survived many assassination attempts and rebellions. They craved peace.

The play is full of many examples of nature reflecting the actions of men. When Duncan is murdered, the stars don't even shine. They are a source of light that comes from the heavens and therefore near God, and they can't even look at the horrible event that is going to take place. In fact, Lady Macbeth asks for darkness to cover her plans to kill Duncan. "Stars hide your fires … black and keep desires."

When Macduff arrives with Lennox to wake the King, Lennox describes the terrible weather that they have just ridden through. "The night has been unruly. Where we lay,/Our chimneys were blown down and ,as they say,/Lamentings heard I' th' air, strange screams of death,/And prophesying, with accents terrible,/Of dire combustion and confused events/…." Momentous reactions of the natural world to the momentous murder of a king. The Old Man and Ross, in Act 2, scene 4, discuss more unnatural events: "Hours dreadful and things strange, …" The world is dark during the daytime and a "mousing owl" kills a hawk—both the opposite of what the natural order should be.

Clothing Imagery

Clothing imagery is associated with Macbeth. When he is first addressed as Thane of Cawdor, he asks, "Why do you dress me/In borrowed robes." At this point, Macbeth thinks the Thane of Cawdor is still alive. He doesn't know that Cawdor is going to be executed for treason against his king. (Ironically, as Thane of Cawdor, he is guilty of the same crime.)

In the scene-by-scene, other examples of this theme will be highlighted. It's important to the character of Macbeth that he is never comfortable in his title he has. The imagery reflects this by often describing his clothes as ill-fitting.

Illness, Disease, Madness

In the play, the subject of illness and disease arises frequently after Macbeth has become king. Scotland is described as diseased and Macbeth and Lady Macbeth suffer as well. This topic can lead to an interesting project on Renaissance medicine.

Fair is Foul

This theme is introduced by the three witches in scene 1, and, by no accident, is repeated by Macbeth in scene 2. If the audience wasn't sure that Macbeth was evil, the fact that he says exactly the same words as the witches is enough to make him the villain.

Fair is foul, generally relates to characters and their actions. Duncan thought that the original Thane of Cawdor was fair (a good man) but he turned out to be a traitor. Duncan thought the same of Macbeth. Lady Macbeth urges Macbeth to look pleasant like a flower, but "be the serpent under it." Duncan and Banquo think

Macbeth's castle looks beautiful and friendly, but it's inhabited by the people who want to kill their king. More of these examples will be mentioned in the scene by scene.

Tragic Hero

The tragic hero, based on Aristotle's description, has the following characteristics:

1) The character is of noble birth or has high stature.
2) The character has many good qualities, but also has a tragic flaw. Pride and ambition are popular choices.
3) The hero's flaw affects decisions that he makes.
4) Sometimes the hero realizes what has caused his downfall and reflects on how his life might have been different.
5) The hero's decisions lead to his downfall and death.
6) The audience feels pity and fear at the loss of such a potentially good person.

Macbeth follows this pattern well.

1) He is a nobleman and related to the king.
2) He is a brave and loyal soldier and is described as noble and valiant at the beginning of the play.

3) Macbeth's flaw is his "vaulting ambition."
4) Macbeth decides to kill the king, even though he has strong arguments against doing so.
5) In Act 5, Macbeth reflects on his life in two short soliloquys that show that he realizes what harm his decisions have caused him.
6) Macduff kills Macbeth
7) Because of those moments of reflection, the audience may feel pity toward Macbeth who could have had a better life. The fear comes from realizing how one fault can turn a man's life around and affect an entire country. This is something that the audience would fear because of the power that kings held in their time. A bad ruler can have a serious effect on the country and its citizens' wellbeing.

Here's a link that discusses Aristotle's definition of tragic hero and its model *Oepidus Rex*.

http://www.classics.upenn.edu/myth/php/tragedy/index.php?page=oedhero

Here's another link that outlines the characteristics, as well. http://vccslitonline.cc.va.us/tragedy/aristotle.htm

CHAPTER 5

Scene-by-Scene

In this section, I'll be highlighting the key information that your students need to know about the action, characters, and themes as they read through the play. If you have them read the material aloud, it's helpful to give them some ideas of what to listen for (I want you to listen for clothing imagery in this scene. Make sure you note where you see a change in Macbeth's character here. Look for an example of dramatic irony in this scene, etc.) With those cues from you, they will be actively listening to the scene and have a note or two to help them contribute to the discussion that follows.

Plays were meant to be studied "on their feet" but definitely consider how you will handle some of Lady Macbeth's scenes. Students might not be comfortable standing in front of the class saying "unsex me here" or some of her other lines about killing her children. The "unsex me here” line often leads to giggles, too. Leaving some of the scenes “on the page” is okay.

Act 1

Scene 1

War, thunderstorms, witches, and fair is foul.

> Shakespeare sets up the themes in *Macbeth* early. The country is at war and nature is responding with a thunderstorm. The audience will know Macbeth is either evil or in danger because the witches plan to meet him at sunset, so suspense is built for the entrance of Macbeth. The witches say the line, "Fair is foul, and foul is fair," which sets up that theme for the rest of the play. Not bad for less than 15 lines.

Questions

1) Describe two ways in which the scene sets the theme and mood of the play.
2) What is happening in Scotland at this time?

Scene 2

Macbeth is brave and has been promoted.

Once again we hear about Macbeth but don't meet him. In this scene the Captain describes the battle that Macbeth and Banquo have just won for the king. The words that describe Macbeth are complimentary: brave, valor's minion, valiant cousin, worthy gentleman, eagle, lion. Note these descriptors in contrast to how he will described later in the play.

Ross arrives with news that the battle has been won. The Thane of Cawdor will be executed for treason, and his title given to Macbeth as a reward for his bravery--a traitor's title given to someone who will also be a traitor.

Questions

1) Which two generals were victorious in the battle with Norway?
2) Which thane was a traitor?
3) What new information do we learn about Macbeth?
4) To which animals are Macbeth and Banquo compared?
5) What reward is Duncan giving Macbeth?

Scene 3

Witches, prophesies, Banquo, Macbeth's new job, and a secret lust for power.

Witches again. What's important to know here is how little it takes to make the witches angry and how much power they say they have. They say they can control winds and the sea and make a sailor suffer terribly because his wife wouldn't share her chestnuts with one of them. The audience might now truly fear for Macbeth because these powerful creatures want to talk to him, or they might decide that the witches simply have great imaginations.

Finally, Macbeth appears and the first words out of his mouth are exactly the same as the ones the witches said in scene 1. Ominous. If the audience was willing to write these women off as foolish vindictive crones who put on a big show of power but really have none, the evidence of their power is revealed here. They know about Macbeth being made Thane of Cawdor.

Note brave, valiant Macbeth's reaction to the prophesies: "start and seem to fear/Things that do sound so fair?" Why have these words frightened a soldier who has just fought a fierce battle? And note Banquo's statement that the words "sound" fair, hinting that they might not really be fair. Later he refers to them as "the devil" speaking true. He does not discount the possibility that they are evil and can't be trusted. He says this later in the scene, lines 135 to 138.

The students should make note of the prophesies so they can see how they are proved true later in the play.

Clothing imagery is introduced in Macbeth's line, "Why do you dress me? / In borrowed robes?"

In Macbeth's lengthy aside at the end of the scene, we find out that he has already considered killing the king. Note his reaction to the thought of murdering Duncan. His hair stands on end, his heart beats, and he has "horrible imaginings." Compare this later to his vision of the dagger before Duncan's murder and his talk of the blood on his hands after. He has a strong imagination at the beginning of the play that lets him see the possible consequences of his thoughts and they frighten him. This fear recedes later, so it's worth noting now.

Banquo adds to the clothing imagery theme saying that the news of becoming Thane of Cawdor has affected Macbeth like wearing new clothes that don't fit comfortably until they have been worn a while.

Questions

1) Describe two characteristics of the witches that are revealed in the opening of scene 3.
2) How does Macbeth's first line link him with the witches?
3) List the three predictions of the witches.
4) What do we learn from Macbeth's reaction to the witches "all hails"?
5) What is Banquo's warning about the truth of the witches' predictions?
6) What news does Ross bring to Macbeth.
7) What do we learn about Macbeth in lines 133-143. What has he already considered? How does he react to these thoughts?

Scene 4

Duncan is a lousy judge of character.

Duncan's line, "There's no art…" sums up Duncan's inability to see a traitor in his midst and explains why he doesn't see the truth about Macbeth either. A person whom he already assumed was fair turned out to be foul. Duncan praises Macbeth again, building a heroic vision of Macbeth that will be changed by the end of the play when he is called traitor and Scotland's disease.

When Duncan makes Malcolm his successor, Macbeth realizes that the only way for him to become king is to find a way to "o'erleap" that obstacle because it stands in his way.

Natural order imagery is part of Macbeth's last lines. What he's considering doing can only be done in the dark. The stars have to go out to make it black enough for his evil plan. Light = good. Dark = evil.

Questions

1) In Duncan's lines beginning "There's no art …", what characteristics of Duncan's personality are revealed?
2) What words does Duncan use to describe Macbeth?
3) Who is the heir to Duncan's throne?
4) What is Macbeth's reaction to finding out that Malcolm will be the next king?

Scene 5

Lady Macbeth is no lady.

We've just met strong, brave and evil Macbeth and now we meet his wife who thinks that Macbeth might not be brave or evil enough to kill the king. In the natural order, the woman should be weaker than the man, and here is Lady Macbeth wanting Macbeth to come home so she can push him to murder because he might not do it himself. Before he arrives, she asks evil spirits to take away any of her womanly weakness and fill her up instead with "direst cruelty." She, like Macbeth, asks for darkness, "thick night" to hide their deeds from heaven.

She is the one who says that Duncan will be murdered that night. She brings back the fair is foul theme telling Macbeth to "Look like th'innocent flower/But be the serpent under 't.

Questions

1) According to Lady Macbeth, what is Macbeth's weakness?
2) What unnatural demand does Lady Macbeth make on the "spirits that tend on mortal thoughts?"

3) How are Lady Macbeth's words and actions contrary to the chain of being.
4) Why does Lady Macbeth ask, "Come thick night …?"
5) Which theme is referred to in "Look like the innocent flower but be the serpent under it."?

Scene 6

Duncan is no judge of castles either.

This scene begins with a moment of dramatic irony as Banquo and Duncan describe the beauty of Macbeth's castle, when we know that Duncan will be murdered there.

Duncan refers to Macbeth's love of him—also ironic, and these lines also show again that Duncan cannot read a man's character.

Macbeth does not greet Duncan, which is unusual as host of the house. Your students might want to write a soliloquy for Macbeth that he could say while standing at a window watching his wife meet Duncan. The soliloquy would explain why he doesn't greet the king.

Questions

1) What does Banquo's and Duncan's description of Macbeth's castle tell us about their characters? What theme is being referred to here?
2) Explain why Duncan's description of Macbeth's castle is an example of dramatic irony?

Scene 7

Macbeth is a bad host, kinsman, and subject, and Lady Macbeth has a plan.

Macbeth would like to get the whole thing over with, but he has doubts. On one side, he's Duncan's host, a relative and his subject, and Duncan is a virtuous king. On the other, he suffers from "vaulting ambition."

Macbeth's protest to Lady Macbeth includes another allusion to clothing when he says he'd like to wear the "golden opinions" that he's received while they are still in their "newest gloss." Lady Macbeth says that Macbeth is not manly and once again goes against nature saying how she could kill her own child if she had sworn to do it as Macbeth had sworn to kill the king. She encourages him to be brave and explains her plan to get Duncan's guards drunk so that Macbeth can kill Duncan with their daggers, causing them to be blamed for the crime. The chapter ends with another fair is foul quote: "…mock the time with fairest show / False face must hide what the false heart doth know."

Questions

1) What reasons does Macbeth list for not killing Duncan?
2) What is the one reason he offers in favour of killing Duncan?
3) What is Lady Macbeth's attitude toward Macbeth's dithering? Give examples from the text.
4) What is Lady Macbeth's plan for the murder of Duncan?
5) Find the reference to *fair is foul* in this scene.
6) Based upon what you know about the characters of Lady Macbeth and Macbeth, speculate on what you think might happen before, during and after the murder of Duncan.

Act 2

Scene 1

Banquo has dreams, Macbeth sees a dagger, and there are no stars.

We meet Banquo's son, Fleance, and these two characters set the scene for the dark night that Macbeth and Lady Macbeth wanted in order to kill the king. "There's husbandry in heaven; / Their candles are all out." Natural order again—the heavens can't look at such a horrible deed.

After Macbeth agrees to meet Banquo later to talk about the witches, he is alone on stage and sees an imaginary dagger leading him to kill Duncan—Macbeth's imagination again. Macbeth realizes that if he keeps talking he will never act, so he stops vacillating and heads to Duncan's chamber. Note Macbeth's activity of thinking about an action before he commits it because this will change later.

Questions

1) How does Banquo describe the night sky? Why is this description important?
2) What gift has Duncan given to Lady Macbeth?

3) What does Macbeth see before he goes to murder Duncan?
4) What does Macbeth mean when he says, "Words to the heat of deed to cold breath gives."?

Scene 2

Blood and hand washing

Lady Macbeth is still worried that Macbeth might not have gone through with it. She says she would have killed Duncan herself, if he hadn't looked like her father.

Macbeth arrives, shaken by what he has done. The fast interchange of one word lines is written so that there is no pause between them—rushed, urgent, frightened.

Macbeth describes the words of the guards and the curse that "Macbeth shall sleep no more." Throughout this scene Lady Macbeth tells him not to worry about what he's done. She says if they think about it, they will go mad. This is ironic, because she actually does go mad later. Macbeth is too weak to return the daggers so Lady Macbeth does it for him.

Note their reactions to the blood on their hands. Macbeth says the blood on his hands will turn the ocean red, and she says that “a little water” will wash the blood away. His imagination vs. her practicality. This turns out to be ironic as well when Lady Macbeth goes mad and sleepwalks trying to wash the blood from her hands later in the play.

Questions

1) Why didn't Lady Macbeth kill Duncan herself?
2) What word could Macbeth not say to the sleeping men?
3) What does Lady Macbeth say will happen if they think too much about what they have done?
4) What curse does Macbeth think he has heard after murdering Duncan?
5) Why does Macbeth refuse to return to Duncan's room?
6) Compare the reactions of Macbeth and Lady Macbeth to the blood on their hands?

Scene 3

The porter is drunk, Macduff finds the body, Macbeth kills the guards, Malcolm and Donalbain run away in case they're next.

The porter's scene serves a couple of purposes: to break up the tension in the play and to give Macbeth and Lady Macbeth time to change their costumes. The humour needs too much explanation to have any hope of amusing the students, but they'll probably like his explanation of the three things that drink provokes.

Natural order – Lennox's description of the terrible storm and earthquakes shows nature's sympathy with what has been done to Duncan. Macbeth's line, "Twas a rough night," is pretty anticlimactic, and depending on the mood you're in, rather funny.

Lady Macbeth's reaction to hearing the news is odd, too, "What in our house?" It looks as though her plan is successful when Lennox suspects the guards right away, but then Macbeth reveals that he has killed them. When asked for his reasons, his response is full of over-the-top descriptions of dead Duncan and his love for his king. Before he gets too carried away, Lady Macbeth conveniently faints.

Malcolm and Donalbain fear that they will be next "There's daggers in men's smiles."

Donalbain runs away to Ireland, and Malcolm goes to England.

Questions

1) Explain two purposes for the porter's scene?
2) Lines 56 to 65 refer to which theme in the play?
3) What has happened to Duncan's guards?
4) Why do Donalbain and Malcolm decide to run away? Where do they go?

Scene 4

Horse eats horse. Malcolm and Donalbain are accused. Malcolm skips the coronation.

The disruption of the natural order is repeated at the beginning of this scene. "…the heaven's, as troubled with man's act…."

Through Macduff and Ross, we learn that Malcolm and Donalbain are suspected of being behind Duncan's murder "Gainst nature still!" and that Macbeth is going to be the new king.

Macduff doesn't go to the coronation and hints that he hopes it works out in case people realize they were happier with Duncan than they are with Macbeth. Clothing imagery – "Lest our old robes sit easier than our new."

Questions

1) How has nature reacted to Duncan's death?
2) What is going to happen at Scone?
3) Which thane is not going to the coronation?

ACT 3

Scene 1

Banquo has doubts. Macbeth has a plan.

Banquo suspects that Macbeth has played "most foully" for the crown, but is still hopeful about the future the witches predicted for him. He and Fleance go for a ride before the banquet.

Macbeth's speech explains why he plans to kill Banquo. Macbeth has no children ("fruitless crown" "barren scepter") and he's afraid that he's killed Duncan only to make Banquo's prophesy come true. He meets with his two murderers, whom he has clearly encouraged to find reasons to hate Banquo, and they agree to kill both Banquo and Fleance that night.

Questions

1) What does Banquo suspect about how Macbeth became king?
2) Why does Macbeth fear Banquo and what does he propose to do?
3) How has Macbeth convinced the murders to kill Banquo? Whom else are they order to kill?

Scene 2

Lady Macbeth isn't sleeping. Macbeth isn't sleeping. Macbeth keeps a secret.

Lady Macbeth realizes how unhappy they are even though they got what they wanted. She tries to encourage Macbeth not to dwell on it. "What's done is done."

Macbeth envies Duncan's sleep and his peace, whereas he describes his mind as being tortured, and later in the scene "full of scorpions." Lady Macbeth again encourages him to appear happy with his guests and hide his misery. Fair is foul. Macbeth hints at what he's planning to do but keeps it a secret from Lady Macbeth, assuming she'll praise him for it later.

Until now, he has included her in his plans, so this is the first time he keeps something from her.

Natural order – Macbeth once again asks for the night to be really dark while Banquo and Fleance are murdered.

Questions

1) What change do you notice in the relationship between Macbeth and Lady Macbeth?
2) What problem is spoiling their happiness now that Macbeth is king?

Scene 3

Banquo dies. Fleance flees.

Where did the third murderer come from? Is it one of Macbeth's loyal soldiers sent to make sure that the two murderers do their job? Good question for the class.

That's about it really.

Question

1) What happens to Banquo and Fleance?

Scene 4

Macbeth sees Banquo's ghost. Lady Macbeth doesn't. No one gets dinner.

Macbeth is not happy that Fleance has escaped, but is relieved that, at least, Banquo is dead.

This scene is full of irony. Macbeth wishes that Banquo were at the feast, when the audience has just seen his ghost enter and sit at the table. After he sees the ghost, Lady Macbeth does her best to keep the party going and scolds Macbeth for not being manly and having too vivid an imagination. She finally sends the lords away so she can deal with Macbeth. Have the students look at the lines that Macbeth says to the ghost. What person do the lords think he is talking about? They don't know that Banquo is dead, yet.

Macbeth has noticed Macduff's absence and we know that that is not good for Macduff. We also learn that Macbeth has spies in all of his lord's homes. Macbeth decides to see the witches again.

Lady Macbeth says his is so upset because he has not had any sleep. He was told that he had murdered sleep when he killed Duncan. Your students might want to research the effects of sleep deprivation and see how those symptoms apply to the way the Macbeth is behaving.

At the end of the scene, Macbeth shows a different reaction to blood from his reaction after the murder. He pictures himself wading in blood (all of his murders) and that turning back would be as hard as moving forward, so he decides to move forward in his murders. He talks about acting on the "strange things" he has in his head before he thinks ("ere they may be scanned") about them too much. It is ominous that after talking about the missing Macduff, Macbeth ends the scene by saying, "We are yet but young in deed." More murders to come.

Questions

1) What is ironic about Macbeth's lines 41-42?
2) To what incident does Lady Macbeth compare Macbeth's seeing of the ghost?
3) What has Macbeth noticed about Macduff? How does Macbeth get his information?
4) Whom is Macbeth going to see and why?
5) What is significant about Lady Macbeth's comment, "You lack the season of all natures, sleep."
6) What does Macbeth mean when he says, "We are yet but young in deed?"

Scene 5

Witches don't add anything to the play.

Since there's a good chance that this wasn't even written by Shakespeare and was added later. Skip it.

Scene 6

Macduff goes to England. Scotland suffers.

Lennox and another lord reveal that Macduff has gone to England to encourage Malcolm to come back to Scotland and wage war against Macbeth. Lennox and the lord hope that Macduff is successful and that he will return to help their "suffering country/Under a hand accursed."

Questions

1) How has Macduff annoyed Macbeth?
2) Who is Macbeth described by Lennox and the Lord? How does this contrast with the way Macbeth was described earlier in the play?

Act 4

Scene 1

More prophesies, thumbs are pricking, Macbeth plans revenge.

This scene shows how far from being a good man that Macbeth has fallen. The witches even describe him as wicked. "By the pricking of my thumbs, / Something wicked this way comes." This description is a far cry from the brave and noble man of Act 1. He is so evil that he now "conjures" instead of the witches. He doesn't want to hear their voices; he wants to hear their masters, who would likely be even more evil. Once again, have the students make a note of the three prophesies by the three apparitions, so they can see how they turn out later. Note, too, in the "show of eight kings" that King James is one of the descendants of Banquo. Shakespeare has to pay the bills, after all.

Irony – Macbeth says of the witches, "Damned all those that trust them!"

Macbeth's aside reveals two important things. Macbeth is going no longer going to think a lot before he does something; instead, as soon as he gets the idea, he is going to act. Macbeth has been told that Macduff has gone to England, so he is going to attack Macduff's castle and kill his wife and children.

Questions

1) How does the second witch describe Macbeth?
2) How has Macbeth become more like the witches?
3) What are the three declarations of the three apparitions?
4) What is ironic about Macbeth's statement: "And damned all those that trust them?"
5) What is Macbeth's reaction to Lennox's news?
6) What change does Macbeth decide to make to his character?

Scene 2

Lady Macduff and her children are murdered.

The scene is a very domestic one with a wife annoyed at her husband leaving his family defenseless while he is away in England. She doesn't think it is natural for a parent to leave a family undefended and has a chat with her child about traitors. When she learns the castle is under attack, she says she should be safe because she has done no harm. Then she remembers that she is “in this earthly world” where being good can be dangerous. Her son is murdered and she runs from the stage chased by murderers.

Lady Macduff, in one way, represents all good people who are, through no fault of their own, destroyed by other people’s ambition and evil. Shakespeare’s audience would have memories of family members lost to war or rebellion when they were innocent themselves. A reminder that war is not just fought by soldiers.

Question

1) Why is Lady Macduff angry at Macduff? Do you think she is justified?

Scene 3

Malcolm tests Macduff’s loyalty. Macduff learns his family are dead.

This is a really long scene, and I always feel sorry for the actor that plays Malcolm. Directors often cut portions of this scene, for which the actor playing Malcolm is likely grateful. After the high energy that precedes it, the conversation between Malcolm and Macduff is almost too quiet

Nearly 200 lines into the scene, Ross shows up with news of Scotland and the death of Macduff's wife and children. Have the students note Macduff's grief at hearing of the death of his family as it is in direct contrast to Macbeth's reaction later when he hears that Lady Macbeth is dead. Malcolm encourages Macduff to turn his grief into action and help him raise an army to defeat Macbeth. The noble Macbeth of Act 1 is now referred to as a "fiend."

Questions

1) What is ironic about Macduff's line, "Each new morn/New widows howl …"?
2) Why does Malcolm pretend that he has so many terrible faults and that he would be a very bad king?
3) What news does Ross bring to Macduff? Note Macduff's reaction as it will be compared to Macbeth's reaction in a similar situation later in the play.

ACT 5

Scene 1

Blood and hand washing - Part 2

A gentlewoman and a doctor watch Lady Macbeth as she walks in her sleep. Lady Macbeth said, after Duncan's death, that a "little water" would clear them of "the deed." Ironically, in her dreams she can't get the blood off her hands no matter how often she washes them. The doctor and the gentlewoman can both guess at what Lady Macbeth is so upset about. Natural order "Unnatural deeds/Do breed unnatural troubles." The doctor concludes that she needs "the divine" more than she needs a doctor.

Questions

1) What is ironic about Lady Macbeth's actions in this scene? Refer to Act 2 Scene 2.
2) To what theme do the doctor's lines refer: "Unnatural deeds/Do breed unnatural troubles"?

Scene 2

Dunsinane, Birnam Wood

Several lords gather to talk about the upcoming battle. The audience learns that Macbeth is fortifying Dunsinane and that the armies are going to gather at Birnam Wood. Audience will wonder now how the first apparition's prophesy will come true.

We also learn that Macbeth is considered mad by many and that many of his soldiers have left him. Once again, clothing imagery describes Macbeth's state: "Now does he feel his title / Hang loose about him, like a giant's robe / Upon a dwarfish thief." "He cannot buckle his distempered cause / Within the belt of rule."

Questions

1) Where are Malcolm and the armies assembling?
2) What theme is referred to in Angus' lines: "Now does he feel his title/Hang loose about him, like a giant's robe/Upon a dwarfish thief"?

Scene 3

Macbeth is outnumbered. Macbeth prepares for battle.

The scene opens with a Macbeth declaring his faith in the prophesies of the apparitions. He cannot imagine how they could come true. Soon, though, he has a quiet moment when he reflects on what his life has become and how far it is from what he hoped. However, the brave soldier from Act 1 emerges in his determination to fight until the end. He calls for his armor, the one set of clothes that apparently still fit.

When the doctor comes to tell him that Lady Macbeth is ill, Macbeth asks if he can cure her, but the doctor explains that it is her mind that is diseased, and for that, she must cure herself. Macbeth asks him for a cure for the country. In the previous act, Malcolm, Macduff and the nobles all referred to Scotland as diseased. They saw Macbeth as the cause. Macbeth says he wants his country purged of Malcolm and the English soldiers.

Questions

1) How does Macbeth feel about his life now?
2) What part of this scene reminds us of Macbeth as he was before the murder?

3) Macbeth wants a cure for Scotland's disease. What does he think the disease is? What does Malcolm think it is?

Scene 4

Malcolm's battle plan

Using branches cut from the forest, Malcolm's army will hide their numbers until close enough to Dunsinane to reveal themselves for the attack. Prophesy #1.

Question

1) What is Malcolm's battle plan?

Scene 5

Lady Macbeth dies. Birnam Wood moves.

When Macbeth hears the women cry, he remembers when he was the kind of person who could have been frightened by such things. He sees the change that the audience has been watching happen for the past four acts: he is a person who has "supped full with horrors."

His reaction to Lady Macbeth's death should be contrasted to Macduff's reaction to the death of his family.

The soliloquy that her death inspires is probably the most famous and most quoted from the play. Macbeth shares briefly his bitterness at how far he has fallen and how empty his life is now. It would be hard to consider him a tragic hero if not for these moments of self-knowledge that remind us that he was indeed a hero who through his fault of ambition has fallen to an empty end.

Macbeth is told that Birnam Wood is moving, and curses the "fiend / That lies like truth." He is trapped and tired of living but is determined to die like the brave soldier he used to be. "At least we'll die with harness on our back."

Questions

1) How does Macbeth behave in front of his soldiers?
2) Why is Macbeth no longer afraid of strange noises in the night?
3) Compare Macbeth's reaction to hearing of the death of his wife to Macduff's.

Scene 6

Macduff and Malcolm give orders.

> Siward's son is introduced just in time to be killed in the next scene.

Scene 7

Young Siward dies. Macduff chases Macbeth. The battle is nearly won.

> That's it really.

Scene 8

Macduff kills Macbeth. Malcolm is made king.

> Macbeth meets Macduff and says he's been dreading meeting him because of what he has done to Macduff's family. He boasts that Macduff can't harm him because of the prophesy. Macduff reveals that he was born by caesarian section, and therefore not "born." Macbeth considers not fighting, but when Macduff describes how he will be treated, Macbeth says he'll never bow to Malcolm and instead will fight until "the last." They fight their way off stage.

When all the lords are assembled, Macduff returns with Macbeth's head on a stick. I can't imagine how they did this in Elizabethan times, when the average person in London could have had a lot of experience seeing the real thing in everyday life. In theatrical productions I've seen, it's been handled in a couple of ways: one, with a decent replica of the actor's head covered in blood, and, two, a not-very-successful decision to have a lump of something covered in burlap with blood on it. For a student audience, this is often a humorous highlight in the show.

Malcolm is declared king. He promises to bring back the good people who escaped Macbeth and punish those who followed him. He also reveals that Lady Macbeth actually committed suicide.

Questions

1) To what final hope is Macbeth clinging when he is forced to fight Macduff?
2) Initially, why does Macbeth not want to fight Macduff?
3) What does Macduff say to eliminate Macbeth's hope?
4) How does Malcolm plan to get the country back to order?

CHAPTER 6

Journal Prompts for *Macbeth*

Here are some ideas for journal prompts for *Macbeth*, including some ideas for writing the missing scenes in the play.

1. Do you think you are a good judge of character? Why or why not?

2. If you believe in witches and witchcraft, describe these people and the powers you believe they have.

3. Do you believe in ghosts? Why or why not?

4. Describe your worst nightmare.

5. Have you, or someone you know, ever decided *not* to follow the crowd? What happened?

6. If you were going to direct this play, what would you have the witches look like? Explain your choices.

7. Have you, or do you know anyone who has, predicted something that came true in the future? What happened?

8. What do you think are the keys to a successful marriage?

9. What are the characteristics of a good leader? Do you know of someone who has these characteristics? Who is it?

10. Have you ever made a promise that you wished you could back out of? What happened?

11. Have you ever had to tell "not-quite-the-truth" to prevent someone from being angry with you? What happened?

I think some soliloquys might have come in handy to answer these questions:

- What does Macbeth think while he hides instead of greeting Duncan? Does he watch Duncan's arrival?
- What does Lady Macbeth think after the banquet where Banquo's ghost appears to Macbeth?
- What does Macduff think as he decides to leave his family and go to Malcolm in England?
- What does Lady Macbeth think after she hears of the murder of Macduff's wife and children?

- What does Macduff think before the battle with Macbeth?

CHAPTER 7

The *Macbeth* Essay

Topics

Here are a few five-paragraph essay topics that you can use for summative evaluation or put on an exam.

Discuss Macbeth as a tragic hero.

Possible talking points:

Tragic hero is a person of noble birth//Macbeth is a thane and general.

Tragic hero makes a decision that affects his downfall//Macbeth murders Duncan

Hero has a tragic flaw//Macbeth's ambition

Hero's flaw influences his decision//the only reason Macbeth offers in favour of killing Duncan is his "vaulting ambition."

Hero's decision affects others//Macbeth becomes Scotland's disease

Deaths occur because of the hero//Macbeth murders Banquo and Macduff's family

The hero pays for his decision with his death//Macduff kills Macbeth

After the hero's death, order is restored//Malcolm becomes king

---

Explain how the theme of Natural Order is used in the play.

Possible talking points:

The theme is used to define character. a) Because Lady Macbeth behaves so unlike the expectations for a woman of that time--asking to be given the strength of a man, having murderous thoughts, telling her husband what to do—she is punished, losing all sense or order in her madness and eventually committing suicide, which is a sin.

b) Because Macbeth moves from his rightful place in the order through killing a king, he loses any balance in his character. Beginning as noble and brave, he becomes the cause of innocent deaths, can no longer sleep, and is finally described as Scotland's "disease."

The theme is used to heighten the mood. The descriptions of the weather and the behaviour of animals after Duncan's murder give the play a sense of danger and foreboding.

Because Malcolm becomes king at the end of the play, the audience leaves satisfied because the disruption to the natural order has been resolved in the rightful king taking the throne.

Discuss how the theme of fair is foul is used in the play.

Possible talking points:

Character:

Noble Macbeth becomes immediately associated with evil when the first thing he says in the play is exactly the same as the words spoken by the witches in the first scene.

Lady Macbeth encourages Macbeth to behave like the "innocent flower" to hide the evil he is about to do. She greets Duncan warmly as hostess but we know she is planning his death.

Duncan's weakness is revealed in his inability to see evil in his own thanes. He trusts the first Thane of Cawdor who betrays him to the Norwegians. He trusts Macbeth who murders him.

Plot:

The prophesies of the witches seem fair and give Macbeth hope, but they turn out to be the source of his downfall.

Other topics:

The role of Lady Macbeth in the play (would Macbeth have killed Duncan without her?)

The theme of disease, illness and madness (on a small scale with Lady Macbeth's madness and on a large scale with the sickness in Scotland because of Macbeth)

Trace clothing imagery through the play (Macbeth's clothes never seem to fit because he is unworthy of them, references to people being uncomfortable with the new crown of Scotland, Macbeth's return to armour at the end of the play—a return to Macbeth the brave soldier, a role he should have been satisfied with instead of killing Duncan.

Essay Organizer

To get a PDF of this organizer to hand out to your students, please go to this link. The following is a very pedestrian example of how the organizer works, but it should give you an idea of how your students can use the organizer to prepare their essays.

PARAGRAPH 1

Introduction: A general opening statement, for example: Shakespeare's play, *Macbeth*, is still being performed for audiences today, hundreds of years after it was originally written. One of the reasons that the play is so compelling is because of the audience's fascination with the character of Macbeth.

Thesis: **Macbeth is a tragic hero**, showing characteristics that the audience can understand because, though he is a hero, he has flaws that the audience can relate to.

Statement of Direction: Macbeth is a tragic hero because he is a noble person who falls from power, he has a tragic flaw, and Macbeth's decision affects those around him with deadly consequences.

PARAGRAPH 2

Introduction tying argument to statement of direction

Macbeth is a noble person

Supporting Details

He is the Thane of Glammis. Quotes in which he is described in noble terms by the bloody sergeant and by Duncan

Summary relating proofs to thesis

Because Macbeth is a noble person, he has an important characteristic of a tragic hero.

PARAGRAPH 3

Introduction tying argument to statement of direction

Macbeth has a tragic flaw

Supporting details

Examples from text-“vaulting ambition”, dreamed of killing the king before he met the witches

Summary relating proofs to thesis

Because of his flaw of ambition, Macbeth is a tragic hero.

PARAGRAPH 4

Introduction tying argument to statement of direction

Macbeth’s decision affects those around him

Supporting Details

Macbeth's decision to kill Duncan and take his throne affects those around him. Examples: Lady Macbeth's madness, killing Banquo and Macduff's family to keep his power, becoming Scotland's disease and nearly ruining the kingdom

Summary relating proofs to thesis

Because Macbeth's decision to kill Duncan caused many other deaths, he is a tragic hero.

PARAGRAPH 5

Recap of Thesis

Macbeth shares many characteristics of the tragic hero.

Recap of Proofs

Macbeth was of noble birth and ambition was his tragic flaw. His decision to kill Duncan resulted in his killing others, including Banquo and Macduff's family.

Summative statement

Since people continue to see news stories about heroes or celebrities whom they have held in high esteem who have hurt others and fallen from grace (Lance Armstrong, Bill Cosby), it's no wonder that Shakespeare's depiction of Macbeth as a tragic hero still resonates with audiences today.

Essay Evaluation

Here is a list of links for rubrics for essay evaluation. Choose the one that works best for you and for the expectations of your department administrators.

1. A great how-to for creating rubrics with examples for essay evaluation

http://www.nuigalway.ie/celt/teaching_and_learning/Rubrics_QG_v1.1.2.pdf

2. For ESL learners

http://www.wcs.k12.va.us/users/honaker/Rubric4c-Writing-rubric.pdf

3. From NCTE

http://www.readwritethink.org/files/resources/printouts/Essay%20Rubric.pdf

4. For Grade 8s

This is a Word document, so it could be changed to match your grade level. It's very comprehensive

https://www.google.ca/url?sa=t&rct=j&q=&esrc=s&source=web&cd=8&ved=0CDgQFjAH&url=http%3A%2F%2Ffhenglishlab.wikispaces.com%2Ffile%2Fview%2FEssay%2BEvaluation%2BRubric.doc&ei=03jLVNHkEMKPyASMmoGYDg&usg=AFQjCNHNy-_KXtHYSZt660p_nshJWWrzBg&sig2=GMXd0E5NWpURGjD-wDqswQ&cad=rja

5. Another Word document that you can adapt

https://www.google.ca/url?sa=t&rct=j&q=&esrc=s&source=web&cd=16&ved=0CDsQFjAFOAo&url=https%3A%2F%2Fonlineteachingandlearning.wikispaces.com%2Ffile%2Fview%2FRubric%2Bfor%2BGrading%2Band%2BEvaluating%2BEssays.doc&ei=eXrLVM6-F4WiyATg54HYCg&usg=AFQjCNFxkyKnOdJ_85HEOrrIFr8xuYK4UQ&sig2=F_0ewxRMBjJOUx6WveTd0w&cad=rja

CHAPTER 8

Online Resources

Rather than reinvent the wheel, here is a list of links you can use to find tests, homework questions, essays, projects, etc. for *Macbeth.* Links to *Cliff Notes* and *Spark Notes* are included because, after all, you may as well know what your students are reading.

1) ***Macbeth* Study Guide at Shakespeare Online:**
   http://www.shakespeare-online.com/plays/macbeth/macbethresources.html - the site features synopses, analysis, study quiz (with detailed answers), comparisons between plays, essay topics, and a discussion of Shakespearean and Elizabethan Tragedy
2) **Teaching *Macbeth,* Resources from Folger Education:**

http://www.folger.edu/template.cfm?cid=2778 – contains teaching modules, lesson plans, notes, links to videos and podcasts, as well as curricula on performance-based teaching

3) ***Macbeth*, from the Royal Shakespeare Company:** http://www.rsc.org.uk/explore/macbeth/teachers-resources/activities.aspx - contains a teacher pack based on exploration of themes and relationships in the play
4) ***Macbeth* Lesson Plans and Other Teaching Resources at Web English Teacher:** http://www.webenglishteacher.com/macbeth.html - contains a collection of lessons plans and teachers' guides, as well as activities, relating to teaching *Macbeth*.
5) ***Macbeth*, by William Shakespeare:** http://resources.mhs.vic.edu.au/macbeth/ - contains background on Shakespeare, and the culture of Elizabethan England, as well as analysis assistance, quizzes, and pages on essay topics and oral presentation activities
6) ***Macbeth* Index:** http://homepages.rootsweb.ancestry.com/~maggieoh/Macbeth/index.html - contains analysis of characters, the "Great Chain of Being," major themes, important quotes and a collection of simple questions and answers about the play.

7) ***Macbeth* on Cliffnotes:** http://www.cliffsnotes.com/literature/m/macbeth/macbeth-at-a-glance -features summaries and analysis for every scene, major characters, quizzes, essay questions and practices projects
8) ***Macbeth:* Study Questions from California Polytechnic:** http://cla.calpoly.edu/~dschwart/engl339/macbeth.html - a collection of in-depth questions examining themes, characters, and links to resources on tragedy and revenge tragedy. Recommended for advanced students, such as AP or IB.
9) ***Macbeth* at Shakespeare*Help*.com:** http://www.shakespearehelp.com/macbeth-lesson-plans/ - contains many study and teaching guides for Shakespeare, from links to websites, essays, articles on individual study topics, as well as lesson plans, and free quizzes for Act 1 – paid services also available
10) ***Macbeth* on Sparknotes:** http://www.sparknotes.com/shakespeare/macbeth/ - contains general info, analysis and plot overviews, as well as act analyses, a quiz, and study questions and essay topics
11) **Shakespeare Resource Center:** http://www.bardweb.net/plays/index.html - contains

synopses of all Shakespeare plays, as well as links to further resources on each play.

If you find this guide of value, please stop by your online bookseller and leave a review. I appreciate your time and your honest comments.

ABOUT THE AUTHOR

Heather Wright is a former middle and high school English teacher, currently teaching business communications at her local college. Her website, http://wrightingwords.com provides inspiration and tips for teen and pre-teen writers and their teachers. She is also a freelance writer who has been published in local, national and international publications. She often works for publishers preparing teacher support material for textbooks.

Made in the USA
Middletown, DE
29 December 2023